CONFEDERATION AND THE WEST

Douglas Baldwin

Weigl

CALGARY
www.weigl.com

We acknowledge the financial support of the Government of Canada through the Book Publishing Industry Development Program (BPIDP) for our publishing activities.

Published by Weigl Educational Publishers Limited
6325 – 10 Street SE
Calgary, Alberta, Canada
T2H 2Z9

Web site: www.weigl.com

National Library of Canada Cataloguing-in-Publication Data
Baldwin, Douglas, 1944-
    Confederation and the West/ Douglas Baldwin.

(Canadian history)
Includes bibliographical references and index.
For use in grades 6-8.
ISBN 1-55388-014-5

    1. Canada--History--Confederation, 1867--Juvenile literature. 2. Red River Rebellion, 1869-1870--Juvenile literature. 3. Riel Rebellion, 1885--Juvenile literature. I. Title. II. Series: Canadian history (Calgary, Alta.)

FC3214.8.B34 2002   971.05'1   C2002-901449-2   F1060.9.B34 2002

Printed in the United States of America
1 2 3 4 5 6 7 8 9 0   06 05 04 03 02

Project Coordinator
Michael Lowry
Editor
Lynn Hamilton
Copy Editor
Heather Kissock
Photo Researcher
Nicole Bezic King
Daorcey Le Bray
Designer
Warren Clark
Layout
Kara Turner

CONTENTS

Before NATIONHOOD

The British acted quickly, and the rebels were defeated, then jailed, exiled, or executed.

Britain gained control of Québec in 1763. It then established a system of government that would satisfy the English and French populations in British North America. Following the American Revolution, a steady flow of **Loyalist** immigrants greatly increased the British population in Québec. Largely due to the influence of the Loyalists, the British government enacted representative government with the Constitutional Act of 1791. However, the Executive and Legislative Councils, not the elected members of the Assembly, controlled government.

The War of 1812 saw the French and British of Upper and Lower Canada unite to defeat a common enemy—the Americans. However, French–British conflict continued. In 1837, in Lower Canada, the elected Assembly was composed of members of the Parti Patriote. They represented the majority, who wanted to preserve their French-Canadian ways. However, the Executive and Legislative Councils were controlled by members of the **Château Clique**, many of whom were English-speaking merchants.

Louis-Joseph Papineau led the Patriotes in Lower Canada, and William Lyon Mackenzie led the Reformers in Upper Canada. In 1837, they rose in rebellion against their existing governments. The British acted quickly, and the rebels were defeated, and then jailed, exiled, or executed.

FURTHER UNDERSTANDING

Representative government
In a representative government, the population elects individuals to make laws on their behalf. The elected individuals represent the interests of the people who selected them for government. This system is more efficient for a large population than **direct democracy**.

Responsible government
A responsible government generally means that the government is responsible to the people. However, as it developed in Canada, responsible government evolved to mean that the government, known as the executive council, is responsible to the representatives of the people. These representatives are elected by the people and form the Assembly. Under responsible government, if the majority of the representatives in the Assembly do not approve of the actions of the executive council, it can force the council members to resign. Then, either a new executive can be appointed by the Assembly, or there will be an election. The elected representatives are responsible to the voters, and the executive body is responsible to the elected politicians. Today, the Cabinet and the prime minister are responsible to the House of Commons.

■ Louis-Joseph Papineau was known for his powerful speeches that inspired his listeners to action.

In Upper Canada, the **Family Compact** controlled the councils. It strongly supported a British system of rule and disliked democracy. Many people did not like the way Upper Canada was being run. They felt the councils were easily corrupted and that the lieutenant-governor showed favouritism to council members and their families.

The British government sent Lord Durham to investigate the unrest. He recommended that Upper Canada and Lower Canada be joined, that responsible government be granted, and that British affairs be separated from local affairs. His report led to the Act of Union in 1840. The Canadas were joined to form the United Province of Canada. Upper Canada became Canada West (now Ontario), and Lower Canada became Canada East (now Québec), but responsible government was not granted. Although Canada East had a larger population than Canada West, each had an Assembly with 42 representatives.

In 1846, Britain adopted free trade and decided to allow its colonies greater independence. Responsible government was granted in Nova Scotia and New Brunswick in 1848. In 1849, the Assembly in the Province of Canada, controlled by the Reform Party, passed the Rebellion Losses Bill, recommending that people of Canada East be paid for losses suffered during the rebellions. The **Tories** and the Château Clique argued that this rewarded rebels for acting against the British government. When Lord Elgin, the governor general, signed the bill, it proved to Canadians that they had the power to govern themselves. Prince Edward Island received responsible government in 1851, and Newfoundland received the same in 1855.

As the population increased, industries developed, and towns and cities grew, the colonies turned their focus to nationhood and expansion to the west.

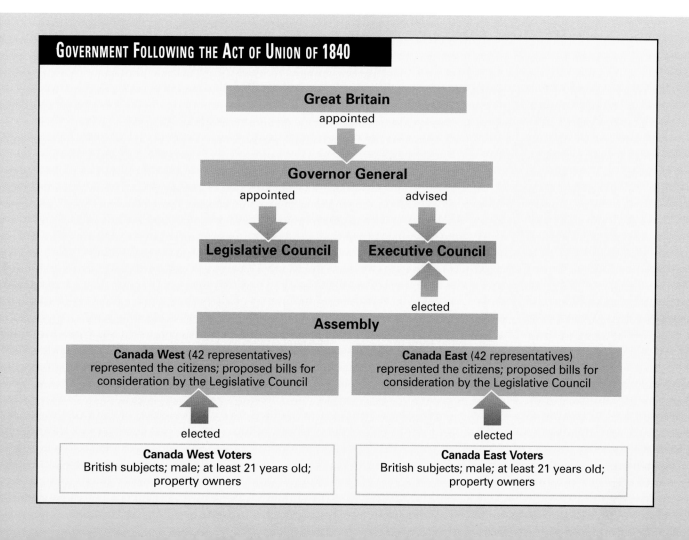

GOVERNMENT FOLLOWING THE ACT OF UNION OF 1840

Great Britain

appointed

Governor General

appointed · advised

Legislative Council · **Executive Council**

elected

Assembly

Canada West (42 representatives) represented the citizens; proposed bills for consideration by the Legislative Council

Canada East (42 representatives) represented the citizens; proposed bills for consideration by the Legislative Council

elected · elected

Canada West Voters
British subjects; male; at least 21 years old; property owners

Canada East Voters
British subjects; male; at least 21 years old; property owners

British North America in the 1860s

The colonies in British North America were largely self-governing by the 1850s. They had begun trading extensively with the United States. Immigrants arrived, and industries grew. While people lived primarily on farms, movement to towns and cities had begun.

In 1860, the population of British North America was slightly more than 3 million. The land between Ontario and Vancouver Island was inhabited by about 100,000 Aboriginal Peoples and Métis, and several thousand European settlers. On the West Coast, 10,000 settlers lived among 30,000 Aboriginal Peoples. French Canadians made up about 33 percent and Acadians 8 percent of the Canadian population.

A Wealth of Resources

In Nova Scotia and New Brunswick, lumbering, agriculture, fishing, and shipbuilding were the mainstays of the economy. The Maritimes ranked fourth in the world as shipbuilders. Prince Edward Islanders maintained a solid economy exporting potatoes and fish. Cod fishing dominated the economy of Newfoundland.

In the Province of Canada, wheat and lumber were exported from the busy Montréal port. Manufacturing included woollen and leather goods, agricultural tools, carriages, and furniture. To the north, beaver and caribou skins were prized items. On the West Coast, the discovery of gold sparked a gold rush.

City Life

In 1860, about 20 percent of the population lived in urban areas. Montréal, with a population of 105,000, had more people than Prince Edward Island and was the largest city. Large cities had gas streetlights and sidewalks made of wooden planks. Most streets were unpaved, and wagons were frequently bogged down in the mud.

Rich and poor people lived on the same streets. Wealthy people lived in large homes with servants, running water, and indoor toilets. Large fireplaces heated each room. A typical working-class family lived in a two-room house with no running water. Their diet consisted of a few fresh vegetables and small amounts of meat and dairy products. Few towns had

underground sewers, and outdoor toilets were common. In the morning, chamber pots were dumped out windows.

Entertainment was forbidden on Sundays. Employers sometimes insisted that their workers attend church. Other aspects of life were quite rough. Prisons and asylums charged admission to see inmates. People bet on horse races, dogfights, and bowling.

Customers had to be careful shoppers. There were no deliveries or money-back guarantees. Most purchases took place only after customer and storekeeper had bargained for some time, even all day.

Goods labelled as "imported" might have come from two blocks away.

Reading was largely confined to the wealthy classes. The most important form of communication was the newspaper.

In 1866, the first transatlantic telegraph line was completed. The Atlantic Ocean crossing now took nine days. Although there were several railways in the Canadas, there was no rail link with New Brunswick or between Nova Scotia and New Brunswick. Snowstorms often delayed trains for several days, and passengers helped to shovel snow from the tracks.

THE UNDERGROUND RAILWAY

The Underground Railway had neither trains nor tracks. It was an informal organization that smuggled African-American slaves out of the United States through several secret routes to Canada. About 30,000 to 40,000 slaves escaped to Canada between 1800 and 1860.

This northward migration began in 1793 when Upper Canada passed a law ending slavery in the colony. By 1833, slavery had been abolished in all of British North America.

Concerned Americans, known as "conductors," began to send runaway slaves, called "cargo" or "passengers," to Canada. Temporary hiding places were known as "stations," and the escape route was called the "line" or "track." Following the American Civil War in 1865, the Underground Railway was no longer necessary, and many former slaves returned to live in the United States.

Josiah Henson 1789-1883   postage/postes

■ Josiah Henson was one of the first people to be a part of the Underground Railway. He founded the community of Dawn near Dresden, Ontario.

POWER in the Province of Canada

In 1841, when Great Britain united Upper and Lower Canada into the United Province of Canada, each of the Canadas had forty-two representatives in the Assembly.

The **Francophones** pointed out that the population of Canada East was much larger than that of Canada West, and Francophones made up about 70 per cent of the population of Canada East. Clearly, the people of Canada East, in particular the Francophones, would be under-represented in the Assembly. They feared that if the **Anglophones** from both sections of the Province of Canada got together to form a single political party, its members would dominate the Assembly.

As it turned out, the fears of the Francophones were unfounded. The party with the greatest number of members elected to the Assembly formed the government. To stay in power, the government had to be able to outvote the rest of the Assembly on every issue put to vote. A group of men in the Assembly might agree to vote together on an issue. When other issues were discussed, these same men might break into as many as a dozen splinter groups, each taking its own particular stand. If even two or three government members voted against their party on a particular issue, their votes, added to those of non-government members, might force the government to resign.

Political Parties

Toward the end of the 1850s, there were four major parties in the Province of Canada. In Canada West, John A. Macdonald of the Conservative Party and George Brown, leader of the Reform Party, were the leading politicians. Macdonald's chief opposition came from George Brown. The men had a personal dislike for each other. When they met on the street, they passed by without a word. In the Assembly, they attacked each other viciously. As a result, the Tory and Reform parties did not join forces.

Macdonald instead allied himself with George-Étienne Cartier, leader of the Parti Bleu in Canada East. By promising to

■ The legislature of the United Province of Canada was split along linguistic, social, cultural, and political lines.

FURTHER UNDERSTANDING

Conservative Leading up to the Rebellion in 1837, the Family Compact controlled the Executive and Legislative Councils in Upper Canada. The compact promoted British practices and institutions. Members of the compact later became known as the Tories—a British term for people who favour conservative political policies.

Reform The Reform Party came into being to oppose the Family Compact in Upper Canada. It was influenced by democratic movements and wanted to see changes in the government. Reformers also appeared in Lower Canada and in the Maritimes. Reformers and Conservatives traditionally have opposing views.

support the interests of the Francophones, Macdonald won the backing of most of Canada East. At the same time, he was able to bring into his party several Anglophone businesspeople from Canada West.

In Canada East, George-Étienne Cartier's Parti Bleu was supported by

the Roman Catholic clergy. Antoine-Aimé Dorion's Parti Rouge wanted to force the church out of politics. This religious split prevented the two French-Canadian parties in Canada East from working together.

PARTY POLITICS

Canada East

Le Parti Rouge (Rouges)

- Led by Antoine-Aimé Dorion
- Wanted more people to have the vote
- Opposed the power of the Roman Catholic Church in government
- Strong believers in French rights
- Wanted independence from Britain
- Elected twenty-four members in 1863

Le Parti Bleu (Bleus)

- Led by George-Étienne Cartier
- Supported by most French Canadians
- Supported by the Catholic Church
- Is against representation by population
- Elected thirty-eight members in 1863

■ Dorion admired American-style democracy.

■ Cartier wanted to cooperate with English-Canadian business interests. He was a businessman himself.

Canada West

Conservative Party (Tories)

- Led by John A. Macdonald
- Agreed to protect French rights and to develop English business interests
- Not as large as the Reform party and becoming smaller
- Against representation by population
- Elected twenty-four members in 1863

Reform Party (Clear Grits)

- Led by George Brown
- Wanted representation by population
- Believed that religion and politics should not mix
- Wanted to expand to the North-West
- Elected forty members

■ The Reform Party believed that representation by population would end French-Canadian control.

■ Macdonald believed in working together with French Canadians to promote the growth of the colony.

Political DEADLOCK

The colony was almost impossible to govern by the 1860s. Petty jealousies, personality conflicts, and religious and ethnic differences resulted in a political deadlock, making it difficult for any one political party to gain a majority in the Assembly. Since no party could hold power for long, the government passed few important laws. Many citizens of Canada West wanted to expand into the fertile farming lands in the North-West, but the French-Canadian members always **vetoed** this idea. On issues such as taxation, education, railways, and where to locate the capital of the colony, many Upper Canadians felt that their wishes were ignored. Unless some means could be found to end this political seesaw, the day-to-day governance of the province could not be carried out efficiently or effectively.

"Rep by Pop"

In 1841, Canada East had many more people than Canada West. By 1861, however, Canada West had more people. Now, it was the Anglophones of Canada West who complained that they should have more members. They believed it was unfair to give Canada East and Canada West an equal number of members in the Assembly.

The Reform Party believed that the best solution was representation by population. It proposed that each section be assigned

■ John A. Macdonald grew up in Kingston, Upper Canada, and was a successful businessman and lawyer before turning to politics.

FURTHER UNDERSTANDING

Coalition Individuals or groups who agree to join together and cooperate to achieve a common purpose are forming an alliance. Political parties sometimes form an alliance known as a coalition. Two or more parties formally agree to work together in order to achieve a common goal. For example, they might agree to vote together to ensure a particular bill is passed. They might work together temporarily in order to gain power and control government.

Representation by population Representation by population is a political system in which the number of elected representatives allowed to each region depends on the number of people living there. The number of representatives for a given region represents the proportional size of their population in relation to the total population. If Region A's population is two times as large as Region B's population, Region A will have twice as many representatives as Region B.

members in proportion to the size of its population. "Rep by Pop" became their rallying cry. Brown took up the cause. Rep by Pop would give English Canadians in Canada West more members and more power in the Assembly. French Canadians of both parties opposed representation by population. John A. Macdonald also opposed Rep by Pop. He thought it was too democratic.

The Great Coalition

A crisis occurred on June 14, 1864, when the Conservative Party was defeated in the Assembly. The Reform Party had been defeated only three months before.

Members groaned as the results were announced. Almost all of them dreaded another election, which would bring in yet another government and the same political deadlock. George Brown rose to his feet in the Assembly to offer his support to any party willing to "consider the interests of both sections of the Province, and to find a settlement of our difficulties!" He said he was even prepared to join the government of his political enemy, John A. Macdonald. For a moment, the members of the Assembly were stunned. Then a solitary cheer broke the silence, quickly followed by many longer, louder ones. The political deadlock had at last been broken.

■ John A. Macdonald was known as a shrewd political tactician who believed in the pursuit of practical goals by practical means. His intelligence and ability were evident during his political campaigns and speeches.

An Interesting PROPOSAL

Politicians in the Canadas hoped that Confederation would provide defence against an American invasion.

During the early 1860s, a union of all the British North American colonies was discussed, but political differences made it seem unlikely. By 1864, however, Confederation received serious attention.

The American Threat

The United States was in the midst of a civil war, and some American politicians were talking about marching north into Canada at war's end. Politicians in the Canadas hoped that Confederation would provide defence against an American invasion.

In 1861, the United States and Great Britain had been on the brink of war. The American navy stopped a British ship, the *Trent*, and captured two enemy agents. Britain demanded an apology and the release of the prisoners, but President Abraham Lincoln refused. For two months, British North Americans feared a war. The Trent affair ended when Lincoln released the prisoners without an apology. The incident showed Canadians the potential danger from the south. Confederation would provide both a unified army and money to build a railway to transport troops.

The Promise of Prosperity

Dreams of economic growth also fuelled the Confederation movement. Since the St. Lawrence River was frozen six months of the year, a **transcontinental** railway would help provide year-round trade.

FURTHER UNDERSTANDING

Confederation The Confederation plan proposed separating the United Province of Canada into two provinces—Ontario and Québec—and uniting them with the four Atlantic colonies. Each province would have its own government for local matters. It would also elect members to a House of Commons in Ottawa according to the size of its population.

Many people wished to extend the new nation "from sea unto sea." George Brown stated, " ... what we propose now is but to lay the foundations of the structure—to set in motion the governmental machinery that will one day, we trust, extend from the Atlantic to the Pacific."

House of Commons The Confederation plan called for the creation of a House of Commons, which would be made up of elected representatives, called Members of Parliament. Together,

the Senate and the House of Commons would make up Parliament. They would be the law-making branch of government. The Confederation plan specified that the House of Commons would make national decisions on matters affecting more than one province.

Transcontinental railway A transcontinental railway would allow Canadians to ship grain and manufactured products to the Maritimes and beyond. The Maritimes could send coal and fish to central Canada.

There were several railways in Canada. The longest was the Grand Trunk, but it was on the verge of bankruptcy. It needed more passengers and freight. These increases would happen if the railway was extended from the Atlantic to the Pacific. The provinces had to be united to build such a railway.

■ The dream of a transcontinental railway was a motivating factor in the push for Confederation. A railway would help overcome the vast distances that separated the colonies.

Confederation would also improve interprovincial trade. This became important when the United States announced its intention to end the 1854 free-trade agreement with British North America.

Finally, Confederation would provide money to purchase the vast area known as Rupert's Land from the Hudson's Bay Company and allow Canadian farmers to move west.

Considering a Maritime Union

Nova Scotia, New Brunswick, and Prince Edward Island had been debating the possibility of a union. Some Maritime politicians and the British government believed that a Maritime union would turn the three relatively weak colonies into a single, more powerful body. The formation of a new colony would save money and eliminate problems such as different currencies and laws.

However, the Maritime union had few supporters. Each province wanted to protect its own rights, and there was only limited contact between the provinces. One Prince Edward Islander complained about the difficulty of sending people to meetings. Would they, he asked, be "expected to take pole in hand and leap from iceberg to iceberg across the Straits in the dead of winter?" The Canadian government asked to be invited to the next Maritime meeting to present its proposal.

■ Prince Edward Island's prosperous shipbuilding industry would be a welcome addition to a united Canadian economy.

The Charlottetown
CONFERENCE

Prince Edward Island agreed to attend a conference if the meeting was held on the island. Therefore, the conference was held at Charlottetown between September 1 and 9, 1864.

At first, islanders displayed a general lack of interest. When the delegates from Nova Scotia and New Brunswick arrived, there was no one to meet them. Everyone, it seemed, was at the circus, which was making its first island appearance in twenty-one years. When the Canadians arrived the next day aboard the steamboat *Queen Victoria*, they were all but ignored. Undisturbed, George Brown wrote that the Canadian delegates "dressed [them]selves in correct style," rowed to shore, and "landed like Mr. Christopher Columbus."

The delegates met in the richly decorated Province House, from which the press was barred. Speeches from John A. Macdonald, George-Étienne Cartier, Alexander Galt, Thomas D'Arcy McGee, and George Brown convinced the Maritime representatives that a union of all the British North American colonies might be a good idea.

The six days of meetings were accompanied by endless parties. Islanders wined and dined the delegates. Dinners included beef, ham, salmon, lobster, oysters, fruits, pastries, and wine. The banquet meal was followed by three hours of speeches. The delegates toasted each other and sang "For They Are Jolly Good Fellows." Cartier concluded the banquet by singing "God Save the Queen" in English and French. The crowning event was a grand ball. The delegates and their spouses danced from 10:00 in the evening until 1:00 in the morning. The next day, the delegates left for a tour of the Maritimes before proceeding to Québec City to hammer out a new constitution.

FURTHER UNDERSTANDING

Constitution The legally binding document and the basic ideas upon which a government is based is its constitution. Governments of the British North American colonies were based upon the British system, which was in great part not written. Canada has a written constitution that is based on Britain's unwritten constitution. Some of the Constitutional acts that have occurred in Canada include the recognition of Canada's independence, the patriation of the Constitution, and the creation of a charter of rights and freedoms.

■ The Charlottetown Conference was so successful that the city is considered the "Cradle of Confederation." In this painting, the Fathers of Confederation dance at a ball at Province House in 1864.

The Québec CONFERENCE

Thirty-three delegates, including two members from Newfoundland, attended the conference at Québec City in October 1864. It rained for the entire seventeen days. One reporter wrote, "What can I tell you? Almost nothing. It is raining. It rains every day, making the stay in Québec—normally so gay and amusing when the weather is fine—disagreeable in the extreme."

The delegates met from 11:00 AM to 4:00 PM every day except Sunday. Smaller, informal meetings took place at other times. After the first week, the delegates also met in the evening from 7:30 to midnight. Unlike the party mood at Charlottetown, arguments raged back and forth at the Québec Conference. Prince Edward Island, the smallest colony, disagreed with representation by population in the House of Commons. Financial arrangements and the number of seats in the Senate were also hotly debated issues.

John A. Macdonald was at his best. His proposal for dividing federal and provincial powers was easily accepted. He was usually able to cool down tempers when discussions became heated. He wined and dined the delegates, as well as their wives and children. An Island delegate noted that "the Canadians are the most tireless dancers I have ever seen … They do not seem to miss a dance during the live long night. They are cunning fellows; and there's no doubt that it is all done for a political purpose. They know that if they can dance themselves into the affections of the wives and daughters of the Maritimers, the men will certainly become an easy target."

After seventeen days of heated debate, the delegates drew up seventy-two recommendations called the Québec Resolutions. The delegates then returned home to convince their governments to accept the resolutions.

> John A. Macdonald wined and dined the delegates, as well as their wives and children.

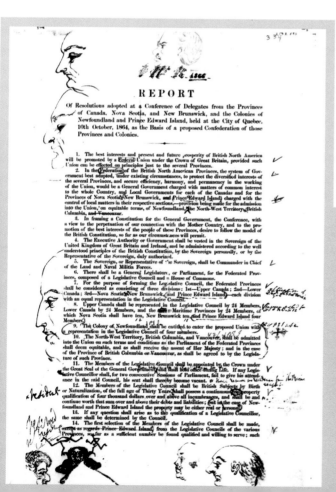

■ On his Québec Conference papers from October 10, 1864, John A. Macdonald scribbled changes and highlights to the seventy-two resolutions.

APPROVAL
in Canada East and West

> "We must either have Confederation or be taken over by the United States."

People in Canada West were the most enthusiastic about the idea of Confederation. It would give them their own province, improve their economy, and encourage expansion to the West. As the most populated province, Ontario would have the most representatives in Ottawa.

French Canadians were not as enthusiastic. Several members questioned whether Confederation would provide protection for French-Canadian rights. They wanted the provincial government to be more powerful than the central government. Antoine-Aimé Dorion, who led the opposition to Confederation, said, "Some people think that by adding two and two together you get five. But I cannot see how, by adding the population of the Maritime provinces to that of Canada, you can multiply them to make a larger force to defend the country." Many French-Canadian politicians had not read the Québec Resolutions and could not understand English well enough to follow the debates in the Assembly.

They relied on George-Étienne Cartier and the Roman Catholic clergy to guide them.

Cartier believed that Confederation provided the best possibility for harmony among the provinces. He stated that "the question for us to ask ourselves was this: shall we be content to remain separate or shall we be content to maintain a mere provincial existence, when, by combining together, we could become a great nation?"

Cartier desired economic growth. As the lawyer for the Grand Trunk Railway, he favoured Confederation as a way of saving it from bankruptcy. Cartier also feared **annexation** by the United States and considered the idea of Confederation the only way to prevent this. "We must either have Confederation or be taken over by the United States," he declared. When the Assembly voted on the Québec Resolutions early in 1865, Canada West approved the scheme by a vote of fifty-four to eight. In Canada East, twenty-six of the forty-eight French-Canadian members voted in favour of it.

FURTHER UNDERSTANDING

Grand Trunk Railway The Grand Trunk Railway (GTR) was formed in 1852 with the intention of building a railway through the Province of Canada. Construction of the railway boosted the Canadian labour force as workers came from Britain. At the time of Confederation, the GTR was the longest railway system in the world. The GTR made world headlines in 1885, when the well-known circus elephant Jumbo died after he charged a GTR train.

■ Delegates who took part in at least one of the three Confederation conferences—Charlottetown, Québec City, or London—were called the Fathers of Confederation. There were thirty-six "fathers" in total.

The Atlantic DILEMMA

Confederation was more controversial in the Atlantic colonies. Each colony had different reasons for rejecting and accepting the proposal of union with Canada.

New Brunswick Backs Out

Because of New Brunswick's location between Nova Scotia and Québec, a union was not possible without its consent. However, Leonard Tilley's New Brunswick government was unpopular, and many merchants and bankers feared that competition from Canada would ruin them. The Roman Catholic clergy did not like George Brown's anti-Catholic reputation and urged Irish and Acadian Catholics to vote against Tilley. As a result, Tilley lost the 1865 election to Albert J. Smith, who opposed Confederation.

Nova Scotia's Refusal

New Brunswick's rejection of Confederation forced Sir Charles Tupper in Nova Scotia to postpone his province's vote on the issue. While Tupper strongly favoured Confederation, most Nova Scotians were opposed. As in New Brunswick, many merchants, bankers, and farmers in Nova Scotia feared competition from Canada. Joseph Howe led the opposition to Confederation in Nova Scotia. He reminded Nova Scotians that Canadians had rebelled against the government in 1837 and burned their Parliament buildings in 1849. Howe believed that Nova Scotia would be overwhelmed by the more numerous Canadians.

> **Many merchants and bankers feared that competition from Canada would ruin them.**

■ Sir Charles Tupper was the last surviving Father of Confederation. He became prime minister on May 1, 1896.

Maritime PRIDE

How could six representatives in far-off Ottawa protect the interests of Prince Edward Islanders?

In 1865 and again in 1866, Prince Edward Islanders voted against Confederation because their needs had been largely ignored at the Québec Conference. The most glaring omission was the failure to provide money to solve the island's problems with absentee landlords.

There was also a growing pride and sense of identity. The island was prosperous. Shipbuilding and the lumber industry were doing well. The 1854 trade agreement with the United States had opened new markets for island farm produce. As a result, the population had increased from 47,000 in 1841 to 81,000 in 1861. The Northumberland Strait separated the island from the mainland and created a sense of isolation. How could six representatives in far-off Ottawa protect the interests of Prince Edward Islanders? The islanders rejected Confederation, which included a last-minute promise to deal with absentee landlords.

Newfoundland Buries Confederation

In Newfoundland, the debate over Confederation lasted from 1864 to 1869. In 1864, the colony was in an economic depression. There had been several years of poor harvests in the cod and seal fisheries. Premier Hugh Hoyles hoped that a union with the other colonies would help solve Newfoundland's economic woes.

The wealthy merchants and the Roman Catholic population opposed Confederation. The merchants had few contacts on the mainland. They sold fish in Europe, Brazil, and the **West Indies**. Their imports came from Britain and the United States. They feared that a union would hurt this trade and raise taxes. The Catholics did not want to risk any change that might endanger their rights. So great was the opposition to Confederation that the matter was not made an election issue until 1869.

During the 1869 Newfoundland election, people opposed to Confederation spread rumours that young men would be drafted into the Canadian army "to shed their blood and to leave their bones to bleach in a foreign land." The cause was also harmed by a return of prosperity. The Confederation candidates won only nine of thirty seats. That night, some people pushed a coffin labelled "Confederation" through the streets of St. John's and buried it in a fake funeral. The issue of Confederation remained buried until Newfoundland joined Canada in 1949.

FURTHER UNDERSTANDING

Absentee landlords Those who own land but do not live on it are absentee landlords. This system of land ownership had been a problem in Prince Edward Island for many years. After the Seven Years' War, the entire island was surveyed. Parcels of land were handed out by lottery to army officers and others favoured by the British government. These owners were expected to settle and develop the land, but most did not. Much of Prince Edward Island was undeveloped, and farmers were unable to buy their land from the absentee landlords.

The councils on the island protected the interests of the landowners. Even after responsible government was granted in 1851, the island could not settle the land problem. One solution was for the government to buy all the land back from the absentee landlords.

Tide Turns in
NEW BRUNSWICK

Several factors brought about abrupt changes in attitudes in New Brunswick. In 1865, the people had not known that Great Britain supported Confederation. However, during the 1866 election, Britain actively pushed for the union. The colonies were expensive for Britain to defend. Confederation would save the British taxpayers considerable amounts of money. For this reason, Britain instructed the lieutenant-governor to push for Confederation.

The Fenian Raids

Perhaps the most important factor in New Brunswick's change of mind were attacks by the Fenians. The Fenians mounted attacks in 1866 on New Brunswick and in several places in the Canadas. Except for a successful battle at Ridgeway in 1866, the Fenian raids were utter failures. However, they convinced people of the danger of attack from the United States, the need for railways, and a larger union for better defence.

In 1866, voters in New Brunswick changed their minds and elected Leonard Tilley and the supporters of Confederation. The Assembly quickly passed the Québec Resolutions.

Nova Scotia Follows

Now that New Brunswick had accepted Confederation, Tupper acted quickly in Nova Scotia. He bribed several members who had opposed the Québec Resolutions, and the Assembly agreed to Confederation.

> **Britain instructed the lieutenant-governor to push for Confederation.**

■ The Fenian Brotherhood took its name from the Irish word *Fianna*, an ancient name for Irish warriors.

FURTHER UNDERSTANDING

Fenians The Fenians were Irish Catholics living in the United States who wanted Britain to give Ireland its independence. Their plan was to capture Canada and return it to Britain in return for Ireland's freedom.

A New NATION

The colonies needed Britain's permission to join together. Sixteen delegates from Canada, Nova Scotia, and New Brunswick met in Britain in December 1866. At the London Conference, they settled the details that led to the British North America Act of 1867. With it, the colonies of Nova Scotia, New Brunswick, and the Province of Canada (now Québec and Ontario), united to form the Dominion of Canada on July 1, 1867. Canada was the first dominion in the British Empire.

The day was bright and sunny almost everywhere in the country. Church bells rang and cannons were fired. Fireworks lit the sky while bands played "God Save the Queen." A newly knighted Sir John A. Macdonald walked to the Parliament buildings to become Canada's first prime minister. In Toronto, George Brown wrote in the Globe that, "a united British America takes its place among the nations of the world." The first Canadian Parliament opened in November.

There was one important matter to settle—a name. In 1864, the Globe asked its readers to suggest names for the new country. Suggestions included: Tuponia, Albinora, New Britain, Laurentia, Canadia, Transatlantica, Cabotia, and British Efisga (composed from the first letter of the main non-Aboriginal ethnic groups in Canada: English, French, Irish, Scottish, German, and American). Macdonald's choice was the Kingdom of Canada, but Britain feared that "kingdom" would annoy the United States. Leonard Tilley of New Brunswick suggested "dominion." His inspiration came from the Bible, Psalms 72: "Let his dominion also be from sea to sea, and from the river unto the world's end."

The Macdonald government faced the challenge of expanding from the Atlantic to the Pacific Ocean. Work commenced on a railway linking the Atlantic ports with Ontario and Québec. In the West, Macdonald bought Rupert's Land from the Hudson's Bay Company.

FURTHER UNDERSTANDING

British North America Act of 1867 This Act was the official written Constitution for Canada. It outlined federal and provincial powers. The provinces received sixteen powers, including control of their natural resources, education, and health systems. All other powers were assigned to the federal government, including postal service; defence; matters of economy, such as trade, commerce, and currency; and the right "to make laws for Peace, Order, and Good Government of Canada."

Cabinet Members of Cabinet were to be selected by the prime minister. The prime minister is the leader of the party with the majority of elected representatives in the House of Commons. The Cabinet drafts proposed bills.

Dominion The name given to a self-governing part of the British Empire, now known as the British Commonwealth.

■ The engraving on the first Great Seal of Canada took two years to complete. The seal is used to mark important documents. A new seal is created for each new monarch.

NOVA SCOTIA, THE RELUCTANT PROVINCE

On the day of Confederation, some unhappy Nova Scotians burned a straw likeness of Charles Tupper in the streets. The *Novascotian* claimed that it "was only sorry it [the likeness] was not in person." The front page of the Halifax *Morning Chronicle* was edged in black. The opening sentence read like an obituary notice: "Died last night at twelve o'clock the free and intelligent Province of Nova Scotia." In the federal elections that year, the people of Nova Scotia elected eighteen opponents of Confederation and only one supporter—Tupper.

Howe's Opposition

Joseph Howe, the leading opponent of Confederation, believed that Confederation would weaken the British connection. He believed that Charles Tupper had forced Nova Scotia into the union. He felt that the people of Nova Scotia should have been given a chance to vote. In the 1867 provincial elections, candidates who opposed Confederation won thirty-six of the thirty-eight provincial seats. These politicians then voted to leave Confederation and sent Howe to Great Britain to ask for permission to do so.

British officials refused to meet with Howe or to allow Nova Scotia to leave Confederation. Some Nova Scotians urged the province to join the United States in order to improve the economy.

Macdonald realized that Nova Scotia's problems would have to be settled. He offered Howe a cabinet position and promised Nova Scotia better financial terms.

■ Joseph Howe was considered a true Nova Scotian patriot. He was able to use his intelligent and witty powers of speech to influence his peers.

Howe accepted. To explain why, Howe wrote, "I struggled for two years to repeal [Confederation] … But I cannot work miracles … All that can be done is to accept the situation, repair the mischief, and make the best of a bad business."

The Confederation DEBATE

The decision to join Confederation was a complex one. Each colony had different needs and expectations. Finding common interests required considerable debate. At the Québec Conference of 1864, all the colonies voiced their special concerns. To prepare for the conference, each province had to decide for itself the costs and benefits of joining with the others.

Canada West
(Population: 1,400,000)

Many people in Canada West feel that the existing government favours Canada East. The Reformers object to what they call French-Canadian domination of the Province of Canada.

- Political deadlock might lead to annexation to the United States.
- Most of the good farmland is now occupied, and farmers want to expand into the North-West.
- Farmers and businesspeople want a railway to the Atlantic Ocean for trade and defence.

Canada East
(Population: 1,100,000)

Canada East is composed largely of French Canadians who have their own language, religion, schools, and civil laws. Only if these rights are guaranteed in the Constitution will they agree to join Confederation.

- They do not support representation by population. If Rep by Pop is adopted, French Canadians will have less influence over government decisions than English Canadians.
- The farmers and merchants want more markets for their goods.
- Political deadlock might lead to annexation to the United States, which could result in assimilation.
- The English-speaking people in the province control much of the economy.

New Brunswick
(Population: 250,000)

Many merchants do not like the Canadian tariff that will increase the cost of imported goods. They favour free trade instead.

- Many people are worried that the United States might attack New Brunswick.
- A railway to Canada will increase trade and provide protection against invasion from the United States.
- The economy of the province is doing well, and most people are prosperous.
- The population of New Brunswick is small, and many people are concerned that the colony will have little influence on government decisions made in Ottawa.

Prince Edward Island
(Population: 80,000)

The island has very little contact with the Canadas and has no need of a railway.

- The British navy will protect PEI from invasion.
- Because of its small population, the colony will have only six representatives in the new government. PEI will have very little influence.
- The colony is prosperous, and people are happy with the status quo.
- Ottawa is far away from Prince Edward Island, and people fear that their opinions will not be heard.
- The government needs money to buy land back from absentee landlords and give it to the tenants.

 Nova Scotia
(Population: 330,000)

Nova Scotia trades mostly with the West Indies, Britain, and the United States, not with Canada or the other Maritime colonies.

- The economy is prosperous. Bankers, businesspeople, and wealthy farmers feel that Confederation will bring too much competition.
- A railway to Canada will increase Nova Scotia's trade in fish and coal.
- Because the British Navy is in Halifax, Nova Scotians have little fear of American invasion.

 Newfoundland
(Population: 120,000)

Newfoundland is isolated from the mainland and has little trade with British North America. Neither railways nor defence are of interest to Newfoundlanders.

- The island was granted its own government in 1855, and most people do not want to lose this independence.
- The capital of the new union will be too far away for Newfoundlanders to have much influence on government policies.
- The people oppose the Canadian tariff that would increase the price of all imported products.
- The island is in an economic depression and Confederation might turn things around.

Westward EXPANSION

By 1815, the Nor'Westers were urging the colonists to leave for Canada.

While the Canadas and the Atlantic colonies headed toward Confederation, westward expansion was taking place. Since 1670, the large territory known as Rupert's Land had been governed by the Hudson's Bay Company. These lands covered the entire Hudson Bay drainage area, including northern Québec, northern Ontario, what is now Manitoba, most of current-day Saskatchewan and southern Alberta, and even a portion of the northern United States.

The Red River Colony

One of the first people interested in settling the North-West was Thomas Douglas, Earl of Selkirk. In 1810, Selkirk bought a large share of the Hudson's Bay Company. The following year, he was granted a large portion of what is now Manitoba and North Dakota. He called the area Assiniboia. Selkirk sent Scottish settlers to the area, and in 1812, established a colony along the Red and Assiniboine Rivers. It became known as the Red River Colony.

The colony did not do well despite Selkirk's efforts. The man he chose as governor, Miles Macdonell, did not get along with the Métis and interfered with the North West Company and the pemmican trade. Although the North West Company fur traders (Nor'Westers) helped the settlers at first, by 1815 they were urging the colonists to leave. Then they burned the colony down.

Macdonell was replaced as governor by Robert Semple, but in 1816, the rivalry between the Hudson's Bay Company and the Nor'Westers flared into violence. A force of Métis working for the North

■ The Red River cart was constructed entirely of wood and was tied together with leather. It could be easily be disassembled and used as a raft to cross rivers.

West Company seized the Hudson's Bay Company forts in the area. This act secured the Nor'Westers' trade route, but Semple and twenty of his men were killed at Seven Oaks. Selkirk arrived at the colony soon after and struck back by taking the Nor'Westers' Fort William. In 1821, the conflict was resolved when the Hudson's Bay Company and the North West Company merged.

Hardships continued to plague the settlers at Red River. In 1818 and 1819, crops were destroyed by **locusts**. A flood all but destroyed the colony a few years later. Selkirk died in 1820. His heirs were not interested in supporting the colony and left it to struggle on its own. In 1836, control of this area was handed back to the Hudson's Bay Company. However, the Red River community grew as retired fur traders and their families settled in the area.

SURVEYING THE CANADIAN PRAIRIES

In 1857, Britain sent John Palliser to the Canadian Prairies to examine the region and determine whether it was suitable for agriculture. He spent three seasons on the Prairies and wrote the first detailed studies of the region's geology, plants, resources, and climate. His report was later used by the North West Mounted Police and the Canadian Pacific Railway. Palliser found that the Prairies contained fertile land for crops and livestock. He recommended that the Canadian government make treaties with the Aboriginal peoples in the West before the settlers came into the area, but no action was taken.

Farmers in Canada West welcomed Palliser's report. They were looking for new land to settle. One of the motives behind Confederation in 1867 was to expand into the North-West. The Canadian government had to act quickly. The American state of Minnesota was also interested in the area.

Assiniboia

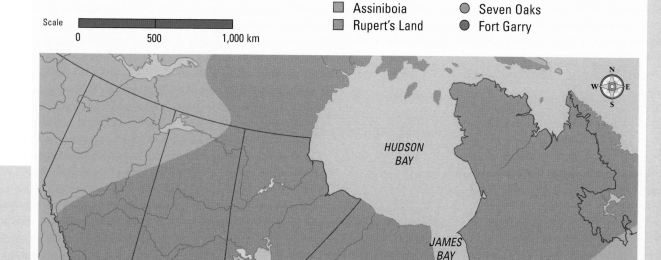

The MÉTIS

Many journeys into western Canada would not have been possible without Métis guides.

There were about 10,000 Métis and 1,600 non-Aboriginals—including Roman Catholic missionaries, Scottish farmers, Hudson's Bay Company fur traders, Americans, and English-speaking Protestants from Ontario—in the Red River area by the 1860s.

The Métis were skilled with horses. They worked for the Hudson's Bay Company as interpreters and guides. Many journeys into western Canada would not have been possible without Métis guides.

Twice a year, hundreds of Métis worked together during the bison hunt. This required great discipline, and the hunt was conducted according to strict rules. The Métis sold the hides to the Hudson's Bay Company.

Red River Resistance

In 1870, Canada bought Rupert's Land. This included the Hudson's Bay Company lands from the United States border north to the Arctic Ocean, and from Ontario west to the Rocky Mountains. The Hudson's Bay Company received $1.5 million, plus 2.8 million hectares of land. The way was now clear to expand to the Pacific Ocean. However, nobody had thought to ask or inform the people who lived in this area about the change of ownership.

Dr. John Christian Schultz was a doctor and merchant who lived in the Red River settlement. He and a small group of Canadians disliked the Métis and believed that the West should be settled and governed by British Protestants from Ontario. He openly supported union with Canada. Schultz and several other Canadians wanted to make a fortune selling land to new settlers.

The Canadians were not popular among the Métis. Although the Métis had been

■ The meaning of the original French word *métis* is "mixed."

FURTHER UNDERSTANDING

Métis More than half the Métis were French-speaking Roman Catholics, descendants of French-Canadian fur traders and Aboriginal women. The other Métis had Scottish fathers and Aboriginal mothers and were English-speaking Protestants. The Métis also had their own language, called Michif, which had developed from Cree, Ojibwa, French, and English.

The Métis learned the Aboriginal peoples' ways from their mothers. Some Métis received a formal education in eastern Canada or Europe. They were at home in a teepee or in a trader's cabin. The Métis developed a distinct sense of identity. They prided themselves on their acceptance of racial and cultural differences. The Métis were well-organized and had their own laws and customs. Important matters were discussed and settled by mutual agreement.

living on the land for generations, they had no legal proof that the land belonged to them. They were concerned about losing their land, customs, language, and religious freedom. The bison herds, which were their livelihood, were also rapidly disappearing.

Although the land did not yet officially belong to Canada, the Hudson's Bay Company let Ontario land surveyors proceed in the summer of 1869. None of the local men hired were Métis. The head of the survey party became friends with Schultz and his supporters. The Métis feared the worst.

Roman Catholic Bishop Taché, one of the leading figures in the settlement, stopped in Ottawa to warn George-Étienne Cartier that trouble was brewing in Red River. The governor of the Hudson's Bay Company and the Anglican bishop also warned the Canadian authorities. Their warnings were ignored.

The Métis had divided their land into long, narrow strips. The surveyors began dividing the land into large squares. Some of the squares ran across the narrow riverfront farms of the Métis. The Métis decided to resist the Canadian takeover until the question of land rights was settled. When the surveyors began to measure André Nault's land, he protested. The English-speaking surveyors did not understand him, so his cousin, Louis Riel, stepped in. Riel announced firmly, "You go no farther." The Canadians left, and Louis Riel emerged as the leader of the Métis resistance.

The Métis formed the National Committee of the Red River Métis with Riel as its leader. Riel insisted that the terms of the takeover be discussed between Canada and the National Committee. Riel declared that the Métis were not breaking the law; they were simply acting in defence of their land rights.

■ The Métis buffalo hunt has been compared to "a light cavalry" because of its almost military precision.

The Métis **RESIST**

The National Committee's first act was to prevent William McDougall, the new lieutenant-governor for the North-West Territories, from claiming the area for Canada. After travelling through the United States, McDougall arrived at the American–Canadian border on November 2, 1869. Here, fourteen armed Métis prevented McDougall from crossing the border. That same day, Riel and 400 supporters captured Fort Garry without firing a shot. This victory gave the Métis control of the entire Red River settlement. Since winter was fast approaching, Canada could not send the military to recapture Fort Garry.

Four days later, Riel invited both French- and English-speaking Métis to a meeting at Fort Garry. A united colony, he argued, would force Canada to grant better terms to the people in the Red River Colony. The people at the meeting drafted a "List of Rights" which outlined their grievances.

On November 16, 1869, Riel created a temporary government for the colony in order to negotiate with Canada on the basis of the List of Rights. The new government's flag, the French **fleur-de-lis** and the Irish shamrock on a white background, was raised above Fort Garry, and Riel became head of the **provisional government.** Everyone in the colony except Schultz's small Canadian group accepted the new government.

FURTHER UNDERSTANDING

List of Rights The Métis drew up several lists of rights, which outlined their demands. The following is part of the List of Rights given to the Canadian government:

- *That the territories of Rupert's Land and the North-West enter the Dominion of Canada as a province. The province, known as Assiniboia, must have the same rights as other provinces.*

- *That we have two representatives in the Senate and four in the House of Commons, until an increase in population brings more representatives.*

- *That all land, rights, and privileges now enjoyed by the people of this province will be respected under Confederation. All customs and privileges will be left to the provincial government.*

- *That every male householder aged 21 or over will be entitled to vote. The Indians will not have the vote.*

- *That treaties will be made between Canada and the different Indian tribes in the province of Assiniboia.*

- *That English and French will be used in the provincial legislature and courts, and all government documents, and acts will be published in both languages.*

- *That none of the Métis will be held responsible for the events of 1869–1870.*

LOUIS RIEL

Louis Riel was born in the Red River settlement in 1844 to Louis Riel Senior and Julie Lagemodière. His father was one of the leading Métis in Red River, and his mother was the daughter of the first European woman to come from Canada to the North-West.

Louis Riel was the oldest of eleven children. He received his early education at the Red River Colony. Riel was a good student and attracted the attention of Bishop Taché. The Bishop sent him to a college in Montréal in 1858 to train to become a Roman Catholic priest. Riel could speak English, French, and Cree.

When Louis' father died in 1864, Riel decided he no longer wished to become a priest and dropped out of school. He worked briefly in a law office and then as a store clerk in the United States. While in the U.S.,

■ Louis Riel is seen by many as the founder of Manitoba and as a defender of western Canada's interests in the new Canadian nation.

he fell in love, but the woman's father refused to allow her to marry Riel. In 1868, Riel returned to the Red River settlement. His talents and his pride in his Métis heritage fuelled his ambitions, and the next year he became the leader of the Métis resistance.

■ Upper Fort Garry was once an important fur-trading post for the Hudson's Bay Company, but with the decline of the fur trade, the fort eventually disappeared.

Macdonald RESPONDS

Macdonald sent two delegates to examine the Red River situation.

When Prime Minister Macdonald learned that Fort Garry had been captured, he postponed the date of the official transfer of Rupert's Land to Canada. He then sent two delegates to examine the situation at the Red River settlement. These delegates had no authority to bargain with the Métis. When Riel discovered this, he refused to let the delegates talk with his followers.

Donald Smith, Macdonald's third delegate, arrived at Fort Garry on December 27, 1869. Although he, too, had no power to make deals with the Métis, he hid this fact from Riel. He explained to the Métis how the government planned to govern the Red River Colony after the sale of the lands.

After checking Smith's papers, Riel agreed to let Smith call a general meeting for January 19, 1870. Despite the freezing temperatures, more than 1,000 people met outdoors at Fort Garry to hear Smith discuss the issues. They met again the following night.

This meeting created a new List of Rights, and three men were selected to carry these demands to Ottawa. It looked like an agreement had been reached. Fireworks exploded above Fort Garry. The three delegates left for Ottawa on February 9 bearing the List of Rights.

■ In 1889, Donald Smith was appointed governor, or chief executive officer, of the Hudson's Bay Company.

FURTHER UNDERSTANDING

Donald Smith Donald Smith worked for the Hudson's Bay Company from the time he was an 18-year-old fur trader until his death in 1914. When Smith met with Riel, he reassured Riel that Métis land ownership would be recognized and offered a pardon to him and other Métis leaders for their actions against the Canadian government. Smith was elected to the Manitoba Assembly in 1870 and drove the last spike in the Canadian Pacific Railway.

Thomas Scott Thomas Scott was a large and aggressive man. The Métis tried him for treason and found him guilty of violence and hostility against the prison guards and the provisional government. Ontario Protestants considered him a hero who died for his cause. His death fuelled their distrust of Riel.

THE DEATH OF THOMAS SCOTT

Dr. John Christian Shultz's general store became the headquarters for those people who opposed Riel. Among the members was Thomas Scott, a 26-year-old Irish Protestant from Ontario. Scott had come to work as a labourer at the Red River settlement. Convicted of threatening his boss with assault, Scott drifted into Fort Garry, where he became friends with Schultz. Both men disliked the French-Catholic Métis.

On December 7, 1869, Riel and an armed group of Métis surrounded Schultz's store. The Canadians surrendered and Schultz, Scott, and forty-five of their supporters were arrested and put in jail for plotting to overthrow the government. Early in January 1870, Riel released those prisoners who promised to leave the colony or to obey the government. A few days later, Scott and several other prisoners escaped. Schultz escaped using a knife his wife hid in a pudding. The following month, Riel freed the remaining prisoners. Meanwhile, the Canadians, led by Schultz and Scott, were preparing to attack Fort Garry. On February 18, Scott was arrested once again and jailed.

After his second arrest, Scott set out to make life miserable for his guards. He constantly insulted and attacked them. At one point, Riel had to prevent the guards from severely beating Scott, who had threatened to kill Riel if he escaped. Riel visited Scott to warn him to behave, but Scott refused to listen. "The Métis are a pack of cowards," Scott boasted. "They will not dare to shoot me."

On March 3, 1870, Scott was brought before a seven-person council. According to the rule of the bison hunt, Scott's disobedience and unruly behaviour were serious offences. Scott was found guilty of failing to obey the people in charge. He was sentenced to death. When Riel did not intervene, Scott was shot by a firing squad the next day.

News of Scott's death caused a national uproar. Ontario Protestants considered Riel a traitor and murderer. They demanded his punishment and condemned all French Canadians. The French Canadians in Québec now identified with the Métis. They considered Riel to be a defender of French and Catholic rights. The country was being split in two.

■ For the English-speaking citizens of Ontario, the execution of Thomas Scott was a symbol of Métis hostility.

The Manitoba Act of 1870

> "No matter what happens now, the rights of the Métis are assured by the Manitoba Act."

The shooting of Thomas Scott turned the Red River Resistance into a national crisis. The three Métis delegates were arrested in Toronto. French Canadians supported the Métis and were opposed to any punishment for Riel. In Ontario, the majority of people demanded that the Métis be conquered and Riel executed.

To end Métis resistance, Prime Minister Macdonald released the three delegates from jail and agreed to almost all the terms in the List of Rights. On July 15, 1870, the new province of Manitoba was created by the Manitoba Act. This province was far smaller than it is today—just a square of land around the Red River settlement. In Manitoba, French and English received equal status as official languages. Catholics and Protestants were given the right to set up their own school systems.

About 607,000 hectares were reserved for the Métis. However, some new settlers were hostile to the Métis and greedy for land. Métis families returning from their summer hunt found new settlers occupying their land. Over the next ten years, more than 6,000 Métis left the Red River area.

To satisfy Ontario, Macdonald sent a military force to restore order in the region. When the soldiers reached Fort Garry after three months of marching, they found the fort empty. On Bishop Taché's advice, Riel had gone into hiding. As he left, Riel said, "No matter what happens now, the rights of the Métis are assured by the Manitoba Act: That is what I wanted—my mission is finished."

FURTHER UNDERSTANDING

North-West Territories On July 15, 1870, Canada purchased Rupert's Land and the North-Western Territory from the Hudson's Bay Company. That same day the province of Manitoba was born. The remaining land was renamed the North-West Territories, and stretched from British Columbia to the Arctic Ocean. Over the years, the boundaries of the North-West Territories were subject to frequent change. The provinces of Alberta and Saskatchewan, as well as the territories of the Yukon and Nunavut, were all once part of the vast North-West Territories.

■ Louis Riel's first provisional government in 1869 was a step towards negotiating the Red River community's entrance into Confederation.

Riel Leaves the Country

The Ontario government offered a $1,000 reward for Riel's capture. To punish him for murder would arouse the anger of French Catholics in Québec. To pardon him would make the English Protestants of Ontario furious. Therefore, the prime minister bribed Riel to leave the country. Macdonald wrote to Bishop Taché, "I have been able to make the arrangement for the individual we talked about. I now send you $1,000. I need not press upon your Grace the importance of the money being paid to him periodically (say monthly or quarterly) and not in a lump, otherwise the money would be wasted, and our embarrassment begin again."

When Riel left for the United States, Macdonald believed his worries were over. Fourteen years later, however, Louis Riel would return to Canada and present larger problems for the prime minister.

■ In 1870, Macdonald sent Lieutenant-Colonel Wolseley and a military force to Red River to restore order. The steamship, *Chicora*, transported supplies for the troops.

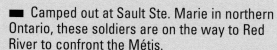

■ Camped out at Sault Ste. Marie in northern Ontario, these soldiers are on the way to Red River to confront the Métis.

TROUBLE in the Red River Settlement

1670 Control of Rupert's Land is given to the Hudson's Bay Company (HBC).

1810 Thomas Douglas, Earl of Selkirk, buys a large share of HBC.

1810 Selkirk is granted a large area called Assiniboia (now portions of Manitoba and North Dakota).

1812 Selkirk sends Scottish settlers to the area to establish the Red River Colony.

1815 Governor Miles Macdonell is not getting along with the Métis and interferes with the North West Company (NWC) and the pemmican trade. The NWC fur traders (Nor'Westers) urge settlers to leave for Canada and burn the colony. Robert Semple replaces Macdonell as governor.

1816 A force of Métis seize HBC forts in the area, securing Nor'Wester trade routes. Governor Semple and twenty men are killed at Seven Oaks. Selkirk arrives and takes the North West Company's Fort William.

1818 Hardships for settlers include crop destruction by locusts. A few years later, in 1819 a flood nearly destroys the colony.

1820 Selkirk dies. His heirs are not interested in the colony.

1821 HBC and NWC merge.

1836 Control of the area is returned to HBC. The Red River Colony grows with the arrival of more settlers.

1857 Britain sends John Palliser to examine the region. He determines the area is suitable for crops and livestock.

1860s Red River is the most populated area in the North-West, including 10,000 Métis and 1,600 non-Aboriginals. Métis are becoming concerned about losing their land and way of life.

1867 The newly formed country of Canada looks to westward expansion.

■ Thomas Douglas, Earl of Selkirk, was an idealist who wanted to create a new homeland for Scottish and Irish farmers.

1870 Canada buys Rupert's Land.

1870 A Canadian survey crew moves across Métis land. Louis Riel steps in to defend Métis' land and emerges as the leader of the resistance.

November 2, 1870 William McDougall arrives to claim the area for Canada. Armed Métis prevent him from crossing the border. Riel and 400 supporters capture Fort Garry.

November 6, 1870 Riel and the Métis meet and draft "List of Rights," outlining their grievances.

November 16, 1870 Riel creates a provisional government.

December 7, 1870 Riel and a group of Métis arrest Schultz, Scott, and forty-five supporters for plotting to overthrow the Métis government. Scott and several others escape a few days later and plan to attack Fort Garry.

December 27, 1870 Prime Minister Macdonald postpones the date of the official transfer of Rupert's Land to Canada upon hearing about the capture of Fort Garry. Macdonald sends a third delegate, Donald Smith. Riel and Smith agree to call a general meeting.

January 19–20, 1871 People meet to hear Smith. A new List of Rights is created.

February 9, 1871 Three men leave for Ottawa with the List of Rights.

February 18, 1871 Scott is arrested and jailed again.

March 3, 1871 Scott is brought before a seven-person council. He is sentenced and shot the next day. Ontario Protestants and French Canadians are divided. Three Métis are arrested upon arrival in Toronto. To end the trouble, Macdonald releases them and agrees to many terms in the List of Rights.

July 15, 1871 The Province of Manitoba is created with the Manitoba Act. Macdonald later sends a military force to restore order, but Riel is in hiding. Macdonald bribes Riel to leave the country.

■ Fort William

EXPLORING the Pacific Coast

Vancouver had completed the longest surveying expedition in history.

In the late 1700s, Spain, Russia, Great Britain, and the United States were all interested in gaining control of the northwest coast of North America. In 1774, Juan Pérez Hernández claimed the Pacific coast for Spain.

Britain's claim rested with Captain James Cook. In 1778, he sailed along the coast of what is now British Columbia in search of a Northwest Passage. Although ice in the Bering Strait blocked his way, he claimed Canada's northwest coast for Britain. Cook was killed by Hawai'ians on the voyage home.

In 1791, Britain sent Captain George Vancouver to map the area and assert its claim to the region. Vancouver had sailed with Cook on his last two voyages. He charted the coastline and explored Vancouver Island. When he returned to Britain four and a half years later, having sailed over 100,000 kilometres, Vancouver had completed the longest surveying expedition in history. He had also confirmed British control over the northwest Pacific Coast.

Overland to the Sea

Both the Hudson's Bay Company and the North West Company wanted to find a practical trade route to the Pacific Ocean. The British government even offered an award to the first person to discover such a route. In 1772, the Hudson's Bay Company sent Samuel Hearne and some Dene guides to look for an overland route through the area the Aboriginal peoples called "the land of little sticks." Hearne did not find a route west, but he explored the Coppermine River and Great Slave Lake. His trip took two years and seven months. Six years later, Peter Pond opened up the Lake Athabaska area for the North West Company's fur trade.

Alexander Mackenzie became the most well-known of the overland explorers. He

■ Before James Cook charted the western shores of Vancouver Island, he had already discovered Hawai'i in the South Pacific, which he had named the Sandwich Islands.

FURTHER UNDERSTANDING

James Cook Cook was an explorer and navigator who had twice sailed around the world. He had served with the British forces that captured Louisbourg in the Seven Years' War. He also helped guide Wolfe's forces up the St. Lawrence River to Québec City. Later, Cook charted the waters around Newfoundland and explored the South Pacific Islands.

David Thompson David Thompson was born in Britain in 1770. At the age of 14, he moved to Canada and began working for the Hudson's Bay Company. After becoming a skilled surveyor, he joined the North West Company and became its primary mapmaker. His exploration and surveys of the West, including his exploration of the Columbia River, allowed him to create some of the most accurate maps of the day. Parts of his "Map of the Northwest Territory of the Province of Canada" are still in use today.

was born in Scotland in 1764 and was educated in Montréal. He joined the North West Company and went to work with Peter Pond at Fort Chipewyan. In 1789, he set out along a river that flowed westward from Great Slave Lake. Although the Aboriginal peoples told him that he would die of old age before he returned and that there were monsters along the route, Mackenzie decided to follow it. He was so certain of reaching the ocean that he carried Russian coins with him to trade with the Russians when he reached the coast. After a very difficult trip, he was disappointed to find that this river emptied into the Arctic, not the Pacific Ocean.

Unwilling to give up, in May 1793, Mackenzie set out along the Peace River to the Fraser River, and then travelled overland to the Bella Coola River. It was an incredible journey. The small party of eight Europeans and two Aboriginal peoples climbed vertical cliffs and shot white-water rapids. At one point, the men threatened mutiny if Mackenzie did not turn around. They finally reached the Pacific Ocean on July 22, 1793. Mackenzie claimed the area north and west of Rupert's Land for Britain and acquired a new fur-trading area for the North West Company.

In 1808, Simon Fraser followed the Fraser River to the Pacific Ocean. He claimed that area for the North West Company. Three years later, David Thompson, another Nor'Wester, explored the Columbia River.

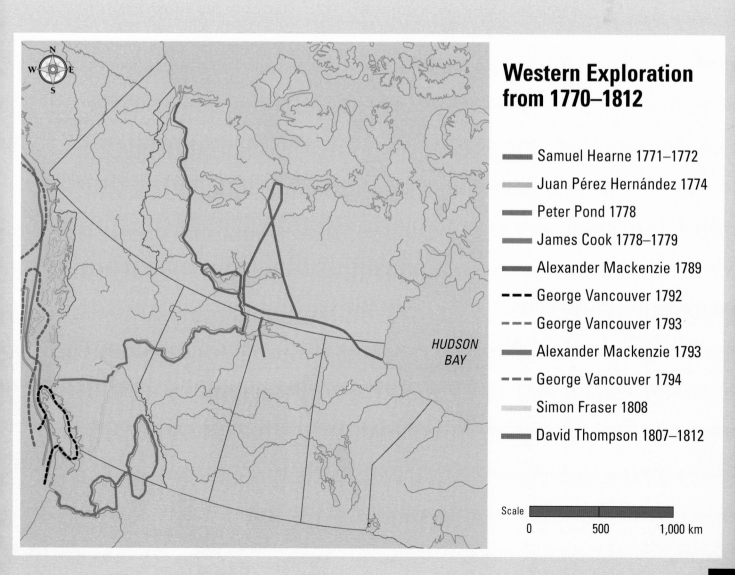

Western Exploration from 1770–1812

▬▬▬ Samuel Hearne 1771–1772

▬▬▬ Juan Pérez Hernández 1774

▬▬▬ Peter Pond 1778

▬▬▬ James Cook 1778–1779

▬▬▬ Alexander Mackenzie 1789

- - - George Vancouver 1792

- - - George Vancouver 1793

▬▬▬ Alexander Mackenzie 1793

- - - George Vancouver 1794

▬▬▬ Simon Fraser 1808

▬▬▬ David Thompson 1807–1812

HUDSON BAY

Scale

0   500   1,000 km

British COLUMBIA

Barkerville grew from a few buildings to be the largest town north of San Francisco and west of Chicago.

Although it had been explored by Britain, Spain, and the United States, there were few settlements on the northwest coast. The Hudson's Bay Company had a few trading posts in the interior and on the coast. No Europeans settled on Vancouver Island until Britain built Fort Victoria in the early 1840s.

After the border with the United States was established along the 49th parallel in 1846, Britain granted Vancouver Island to the Hudson's Bay Company. In 1851, James Douglas, head of the Hudson's Bay Company fur trade in the west, became governor. There were fewer than 1,000 European settlers, and most lived in Victoria. Britain instructed Douglas to create an Assembly on the island in 1856. Since Douglas was opposed to democracy, he set the property qualifications so high that only wealthy people could belong to the Assembly.

The Gold Rush

The discovery of gold along the Fraser River in 1857 turned the quiet colony into a crowded boom town. The first shipload of goldseekers arrived in the spring of 1858. In six weeks, a sea of tents and more than 200 new stores emerged in Victoria to cater to prospectors.

Over 25,000 prospectors from around the world joined the gold rush. To keep order and to prevent annexation to the United States, Britain created the colony of British Columbia on the mainland. Douglas became governor of both colonies. He kept strict law and order among the miners, built roads into the interior, and set up reserves for the Aboriginal peoples.

There were more discoveries in the Cariboo region in the early 1860s. New towns emerged in the wilderness almost overnight. Barkerville grew from a few buildings to be the largest town north of San Francisco and west of Chicago.

While some people made huge fortunes, the colony ran up a large debt from constructing roads and keeping peace. When the gold was gone, British Columbia slipped into a depression. The non-Aboriginal population dropped to 10,000. In 1866, the colony on Vancouver Island was united with the mainland colony to save money, but the cost of governing the large rugged colony continued to be high.

FURTHER UNDERSTANDING

49th parallel In 1844, Britain and the United States negotiated a border between the United States and the British North American colonies along the west coast. Americans wanted the line to be drawn as far north as 54 degrees **latitude**. They formalized an agreement—the 49th parallel would divide British from American territory, with the exception of Vancouver Island to the south, which would remain a part of Canada.

■ Britain was forced to create the colony of British Columbia to accommodate the thousands of prospectors who rushed to the Fraser River and the Cariboo Mountains in the 1850s.

JAMES AND AMELIA DOUGLAS

James Douglas worked for the Hudson's Bay Company from the age of 16. He married Amelia Connelly, the daughter of an Irish-Canadian fur trader and a Cree woman. Amelia was born and raised in the fur-trading posts of the North-West.

Douglas, the son of a Scottish merchant and a West Indian woman, worked for Amelia's father in the fur trade. Amelia helped her husband understand the ways of her mother's people, and Douglas rose quickly through the ranks of the Hudson's Bay Company. He was posted to Fort Vancouver in 1830. Later that year, Amelia joined him.

Douglas was a powerful and intelligent person. When he became governor of Vancouver Island, he ruled the colony with the help of a small appointed council. Once, when the council refused to pass one of his bills, Douglas passed out pipes and tobacco and supplied plenty of wine.

■ Amelia Connelly married James Douglas on April 27, 1828.

He then brought the council together, and they passed the bill.

Amelia had a difficult time fitting into Vancouver society because she was Métis. The British women ignored her. Amelia left the hostess duties to her daughters and rarely left the house. Most of her visitors were Aboriginal peoples and poor people, to whom she lent money and afforded advice.

Prejudice against his wife and himself may have contributed to Douglas's increasingly difficult disposition. In 1863, the British government knighted Douglas for his excellent service, and he retired.

■ James Douglas selected the Port of Camosack for the location of Fort Victoria. The new fort would eventually replace Fort Vancouver as the Pacific headquarters of the Hudson's Bay Company.

British Columbia Considers CONFEDERATION

British Columbia would complete Macdonald's vision of a country that stretched from sea to sea.

Once the Prairies became part of Canada, Macdonald and Cartier turned their attention to the colony of British Columbia. British Columbia was then a sparsely populated wilderness separated from the rest of Canada by the Rocky Mountains. In 1870, the colony was ruled by Great Britain and was populated by only 12,000 Europeans and about 25,000 Aboriginal peoples. The British government and some of the colonists thought that joining the new Dominion of Canada was a good idea. For Macdonald, gaining British Columbia as a province would complete his vision of Canada stretching from the Atlantic to the Pacific Oceans.

With the end of the Gold Rush and the onset of economic depression, British Columbia had to decide upon its future. It had three choices.

1. **Remain a British Colony**
   This appealed to the British governor and his council, most of whom had been born in Britain. These people relied upon the British government for their jobs. If British Columbia entered Confederation, the governor and the council would probably lose their power.

2. **Join the United States**
   This appealed to the American merchants who had come north in the Gold Rush and settled on Vancouver Island. It also made geographic and economic sense. British Columbia had close connections with San Francisco. In fact, there were more Americans in the colony than British and Canadian people combined.

3. **Enter Confederation**
   Most of the newspaper editors, such as Amor de Cosmos, favoured Confederation. One advantage was

■ Amor de Cosmos was an eccentric man who changed his name from William Smith to better capture his personality. *Amor de Cosmos* means "Lover of the Universe."

FURTHER UNDERSTANDING

Amor de Cosmos De Cosmos, born in Nova Scotia in 1825, came to the West Coast in search of gold. Instead of working a claim, he settled in Victoria and founded the *Daily Colonist* newspaper. He used his newspaper to attack the ruling elite. De Cosmos had seen responsible government come to Nova Scotia, and he wanted it accepted in British Columbia. In 1863, he was elected to government. Largely through his efforts, Vancouver Island and British Columbia were united. He helped to organize the Confederation League that campaigned for union with Canada. He worked to make Canada's motto "from sea to sea" a reality.

Public works The government arranges and pays for the development of services to be used by the public. This might be funded by tax dollars. Examples include water systems, waste management, and transportation systems like roads, railways, or canals.

that it would finally give the colony control of its own affairs. One supporter declared, "British Columbia has tried long enough to get on by herself. After fifteen years of hard struggle, she finds herself worse off than she was at the beginning. Her progress has been like that of a crab—backward."

Demands Are Met

In 1869, Anthony Musgrave was appointed the new governor of British Columbia. The British government told him to arrange for the colony's entry into Confederation. The governor won support for the union by promising jobs and pensions to its opponents. He then sent three delegates to Ottawa to discuss suitable terms. Prime Minister Macdonald was ill, so Cartier handled the negotiations.

The British Columbia delegates had four major demands:

1. responsible government for the province;
2. payment of the $1 million provincial debt;
3. a public works program;
4. a road to link the colony with the rest of the country.

Cartier shocked the delegates by offering them even better terms. Instead of a road, Canada would begin a railway within two years and complete it within ten years. The Red River uprising had shown the need for rapid transportation to the West for military reasons. The dream behind Confederation had been to create "a Dominion from sea to sea." A railway would make this dream come true. On July 20, 1871, British Columbia became the sixth province to join the Canadian Confederation.

■ A salute was fired at noon in Victoria to celebrate British Columbia's Confederation Day on July 20, 1871.

Prince Edward Island
RECONSIDERS

Although Prince Edward Island had rejected Confederation in 1865 and 1866, the question of union with Canada persisted. In 1867, Great Britain tried to force the island's politicians to change their minds by threatening not to protect the colony against attack. The island government refused to give in to such blackmail.

The island was remote from Canada, and the islanders did not feel the need for change. The colony was prosperous. Some members objected to the idea of having only five seats in the House of Commons in Ottawa. They also thought the annual payment that Ottawa promised the island was not enough.

Then, in 1868, Benjamin Butler, a member of the United States government, visited Prince Edward Island. His mission was to discuss a trade agreement between the United States and the island. The American government did not take Butler's mission seriously, but Canada did. Sir John A. Macdonald feared that the Americans would use Prince Edward Island as a military base to attack the mainland. The colony was also in a strategic position to control the fisheries and to smuggle goods into Canada.

Macdonald acted quickly. He sent delegates to the colony to talk with the island government to persuade it to join Canada. However, in December 1869 the colony again rejected the idea.

Joining Canada

Prince Edward Island finally agreed to join Confederation in 1873 under the following conditions:
- Canada would take over all the island's debts and operate and maintain the railway;
- the island would receive $50 each year for every citizen;
- Canada promised the island would have efficient and continuous communication with the mainland;
- the island was to be represented by six, rather than five, Members of Parliament in Ottawa; and
- to solve its ongoing land ownership problem relating to absentee landlords, the island would receive a gift of $800,000.

By 1873, Canada was a nation of seven provinces.

FURTHER UNDERSTANDING

Canada in 1873 Canada (present-day Québec and Ontario), Nova Scotia, and New Brunswick joined to create the Dominion of Canada on July 1, 1867. Manitoba joined Confederation in 1870. British Columbia followed in 1871. Prince Edward Island, the seventh province, joined in 1873.

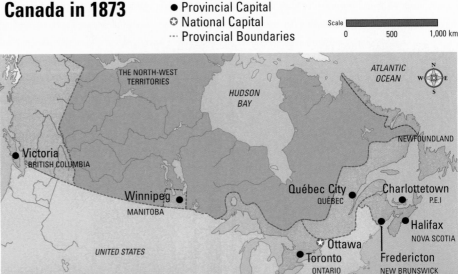

Canada in 1873
- ● Provincial Capital
- ✪ National Capital
- ··· Provincial Boundaries

Scale 0 500 1,000 km

THE NORTH-WEST TERRITORIES
HUDSON BAY
ATLANTIC OCEAN
NEWFOUNDLAND
Victoria
BRITISH COLUMBIA
Winnipeg
MANITOBA
Québec City
QUÉBEC
Charlottetown
P.E.I
Halifax
NOVA SCOTIA
✪ Ottawa
Toronto
ONTARIO
Fredericton
NEW BRUNSWICK
UNITED STATES

THE RAILWAY DEBT

In 1871, the Prince Edward Island government decided to build a railway from one end of the colony to the other. It would be the first railway on the island, and the idea was very popular. Construction workers would be needed, and factories would be built. Farmers could transport their produce to the towns more rapidly.

Railway branch lines crisscrossed the island.

Every village wanted to be connected to the mainline, so the railway wound around the countryside. One-third of the line consisted of curves, and the company built an average of one train station for every 4.8 kilometres of track. As a result, the railway cost far more than expected. The provincial debt increased from only $250,000 to more than $4 million. The lenders wanted their money back, but neither Britain nor the island banks would lend the government more money.

At this time, Prime Minister Macdonald presented the island with another offer. He proposed to absorb the entire railway debt and to provide funds to buy the land from the absentee landlords to solve the land question forever.

■ After heavy snowfalls, train passengers were often expected to help remove snow from the railway tracks.

QUIZ (answers on page 47)

Multiple Choice
Choose the best answer in the multiple choice questions that follow:

1 Which of the following was not one of British Columbia's demands for Confederation?
a) responsible government for the province
b) payment of the $1 million provincial debt
c) a railway to link the colony with the rest of the country
d) a public works program

2 Citizens of which colony buried a coffin labelled "Confederation"?
a) Newfoundland
b) Manitoba
c) Prince Edward Island
d) Nova Scotia

3 Which of the following colonies did not join Confederation on July 1, 1867?
a) Province of Canada
b) Nova Scotia
c) New Brunswick
d) Prince Edward Island

4 Which of the following explorers created the "Map of the Northwest Territory of the Province of Canada"?
a) James Cook
b) Simon Fraser
c) Alexander Mackenzie
d) David Thompson

5 Which newspaper asked its readers to suggest a name for the new country?
a) the *British Colonist*
b) the *Morning Chronicle*
c) the *Globe*
d) the *Novascotian*

6 What year did Newfoundland join Confederation?
a) 1867
b) 1869
c) 1911
d) 1949

7 What were the Québec Resolutions?
a) a document that called for the joining of Upper and Lower Canada
b) a document that outlined the proposed balance of power between the federal and provincial governments
c) a document that proposed Confederation to the Maritime colonies
d) none of the above

Mix and Match

Match the terms in column B with the correct description in column A. There are more terms than descriptions.

A

1. Leader of the Parti Bleu
2. Members of the Conservative Party
3. Opponent of Confederation in Nova Scotia
4. First prime minister of Canada
5. First province created from the North-West Territories
6. A colony plagued by absentee landlords
7. Leader of the Red River Resistance

B

a) Joseph Howe
b) Fenians
c) Sir John A. Macdonald
d) Louis Riel
e) George-Étienne Cartier
f) British Columbia
g) Tories
h) Prince Edward Island
i) Manitoba

Time Line

Find the appropriate spot on the time line for each event listed below:

A Details of Confederation are debated at the Québec Conference.

B Manitoba Act creates the province of Manitoba.

C The Fenians launch raids on the Maritimes and parts of Canada.

D British Columbia becomes the sixth province to join the Canadian Confederation.

E Selkirk sends Scottish settlers to establish the Red River Colony.

F Thomas Scott is executed.

1763 Britain gains control of Québec.

1812 **1**

1841 Britain unites Upper and Lower Canada into the United Province of Canada.

September 1864 Canadian delegates propose Confederation to the Maritime colonies at the Charlottetown Conference.

October 1864 **2**

1866 The first transatlantic telegraph line is completed.

1866 **3**

1867 Canadian Confederation (Québec, Ontario, New Brunswick, Nova Scotia).

Summer 1869 Beginning of the Red River Resistance.

March 1870 **4**

July 15, 1870 Canada buys Rupert's Land and the North-Western Territory from the HBC.

July 15, 1870 **5**

July 20, 1871 **6**

Conclusion

In the 1850s, the Conservative Party was in opposition to Reformers in Canada West. In Canada East, the Parti Bleu and Parti Rouge remained divided. By 1860, political deadlock made it difficult for any party to establish control of government. In 1861, Canada West pushed for Rep by Pop. The Great Coalition in 1864 solved the deadlock.

Threats of American invasion and the desire for a transcontinental railway, interprovincial trade, and expansion prompted discussion of union. At the Charlottetown Conference in 1864, the Province of Canada urged the Atlantic colonies to consider Confederation. Plans were outlined at the Québec Conference. Québec, Ontario, New Brunswick, and Nova Scotia joined in July 1867.

In 1870, Canada bought Rupert's Land, including the Red River Colony, from the Hudson's Bay Company. Louis Riel, acting as the leader of the Métis resistance, tried to defend Métis' land rights. Prime Minister Macdonald eventually agreed to many of the Métis' terms. Manitoba joined Confederation in 1870. When agreeable terms were offered, British Columbia joined in 1871 and Prince Edward Island in 1873.

The Dominion of Canada would continue to push for expansion by settling the West, establishing a police force, completing its transcontinental railway line, and adding new provinces to Confederation.

Further Information

Suggested Reading

Bumsted, J. M. *The Red River Rebellion*. Winnipeg: J. Gordon Shillingford Publishing, 1998.

Creighton, Donald G. *John A. Macdonald: The Young Politician and the Old Chieftain*. Toronto: University of Toronto Press, 1998.

Forbes, E. R., and D. A. Muise. *The Atlantic Provinces in Confederation*. Fredericton: Acadiensis Press, 1993.

Francis, Douglas, Richard Jones, and Donald B. Smith. *Origins: Canadian History to Confederation*. Toronto: Harcourt Canada, 2000.

Internet Resources

Canada: A People's History Online
history.cbc.ca
The online companion to CBC's award-winning television series on the history of Canada, as told through the eyes of its people. This multi-media Web site features behind-the-scenes information, games and puzzles, and discussion boards. The site is also available in French.

The Canadian Encyclopedia Online
www.thecanadianencyclopedia.com
An excellent reference site for all things Canadian. In-depth history articles are accompanied by photographs, paintings, and maps. Articles can be accessed in both French and English.

Glossary

Anglophones: English-speaking citizens

annexation: when one country is joined with another country

Château Clique: a powerful group of merchants in Lower Canada who controlled the Executive and Legislative Councils in the early 1800s

direct democracy: form of democracy where each individual participates in the Assembly and may vote on each issue

Family Compact: group of men who controlled the government in Upper Canada in the early 1800s

fleur-de-lis: name of the symbol found on the present-day flag of Québec; the stylized iris flower was originally used by French kings

Francophones: French-speaking citizens

latitude: distance between an imaginary line, that runs east to west, and the equator; measured in degrees

locusts: grasshoppers that travel in massive swarms, destroying crops and vegetation

Loyalist: an American colonist loyal to Britain during the American Revolution; many Loyalists immigrated to Canada

provisional government: temporary government

Tories: members or supporters of a conservative political group; originated in Britain

transcontinental: extending across the continent

vetoed: rejected a proposal or act

West Indies: a string of islands between North and South America

Answers

Multiple Choice	Mix and Match	Time Line
1. c)	1. e)	1. e)
2. a)	2. g)	2. a)
3. d)	3. a)	3. c)
4. d)	4. c)	4. f)
5. c)	5. i)	5. b)
6. d)	6. h)	6. d)
7. b)	7. d)	

Index